# Introduction

*L Blends Artic Quickies*™ is two photo-based products in one – a reproducible workbook and a CD-ROM - full of handy articulation fun sheets for the busy speech-language pathologist. *L Blends Quickies*™ takes the 28 L Blends photo-words found in the *L Blends Artic Photos Fun Deck*® published by Super Duper® Publications, combines them with 26 more L Blends photo-words, and creates beautiful color and/or black and white activity pages.

Each reproducible book features:

- Thirty (30) black and white L Blends articulation pages (3 each for BL, FL, GL, KL, PL, SL, and 12 L Blends combo pages), plus an L Blends awards page.

- Directions on the pages that allow the SLP to choose the appropriate level of articulation practice – word, phrase, or sentence.

- Name, date and signature lines, so the pages can be sent home for extra practice!

- Perforated pages for easy copying and pocket folders for convenient storage.

Each CD-ROM has:

- The identical 30 black and white activity pages found in the workbook, plus these same pages in **color**. You print out the version that is best for you!

- Six (6) bonus blank "master" articulation pages that allow you to make your own customized articulation pages.

- Five bonus awards.

*L Blends Artic Quickies*™ is the perfect combination for the "on-the-go" SLP!

## Table of Contents

**Word, Phrase & Sentence Level**
BL . . . . . . . . . . . . . . . . . . . . . . . . . . . . . . . . . . . . . . . . . . . . . . . . . . . . . . . . . . . .2-4
FL . . . . . . . . . . . . . . . . . . . . . . . . . . . . . . . . . . . . . . . . . . . . . . . . . . . . . . . . . . . . .5-7
GL . . . . . . . . . . . . . . . . . . . . . . . . . . . . . . . . . . . . . . . . . . . . . . . . . . . . . . . . . . . . .8-10
KL . . . . . . . . . . . . . . . . . . . . . . . . . . . . . . . . . . . . . . . . . . . . . . . . . . . . . . . . . . . . .11-13
PL . . . . . . . . . . . . . . . . . . . . . . . . . . . . . . . . . . . . . . . . . . . . . . . . . . . . . . . . . . . . .14-16
SL . . . . . . . . . . . . . . . . . . . . . . . . . . . . . . . . . . . . . . . . . . . . . . . . . . . . . . . . . . . . .17-19
L Blends Combo . . . . . . . . . . . . . . . . . . . . . . . . . . . . . . . . . . . . . . . . . . . . . . . . .20-25

**L Blends Carryover** . . . . . . . . . . . . . . . . . . . . . . . . . . . . . . . . . . . . . . . . . . . .26-31

**Awards** . . . . . . . . . . . . . . . . . . . . . . . . . . . . . . . . . . . . . . . . . . . . . . . . . . . . . . . .32

# 4-in-1 for BL

**Directions:** Read/say aloud each BL photo-word below. Then, play one of the suggested games. As you take each turn, follow the directions checked (✓) below.

- ☐ **Word:** Say each BL photo-word using your good BL sound.
- ☐ **Phrase:** Say each BL photo-word in the phrase "a ___ card."
- ☐ **Sentence:** Say each BL photo-word in the sentence "I have a ___ card."

*Tic-Tac-Toe* - Players mark BL photo-words with **X**'s and **O**'s. Three in a row wins!
*Lotto* - Helper calls out BL photo-words and player(s) cover(s) them with tokens/chips.
*Cards* - Cut out the BL photo-words. Use them as flashcards.
*Memory* - Make an extra copy, cut out photos, and play matching/memory games.

| blocks | blinds | blouse |
| --- | --- | --- |
| blue jeans | black sheep | blanket |
| blueberries | blackboard | blue ribbon |

Name _____   Homework Helper   Date _____   **BL**

# Who Said That?

**Directions:** Read/say aloud each BL photo-word below. Read each statement in the middle and ask, **"Who said that?"** As you draw a line from each statement to the correct picture, follow the directions checked (✓) below.

- ☐ **Word:** Say each BL photo-word using your good BL sound.
- ☐ **Phrase:** Say each BL photo-word in the phrase "my ___."
- ☐ **Sentence:** Say each BL photo-word in the sentence "___ said that."

**blocks**

"I cover the windows."

**blanket**

"I am given to the winner."

"I am put in a pie."

**black sheep**

"I am used by a teacher."

**blue ribbon**

"I am covered in wool."

"I keep you warm."

**blinds**

**blouse**

"I can make a tall tower."

"I can be worn with a skirt."

**blackboard**

**blueberries**

Name _____ Homework Helper _____ Date _____ **BL**

# Blooming Flowers

**Directions:** Read/say aloud each BL photo-word below. Then, cut them out. As you glue/tape or place each bloom on a stem, follow the directions checked (✓) below.

- ☐ **Word:** Say each BL photo-word using your good BL sound.
- ☐ **Phrase:** Say each BL photo-word in the phrase "___ bloom."
- ☐ **Sentence:** Say each BL photo-word in the sentence "The ___ flower is blooming."

blue jeans

blanket

blackboard

blinds

blocks

blouse

Name

Homework Helper

Date

BL

# 4-in-1 for FL

**Directions:** Read/say aloud each FL photo-word below. Then, play one of the suggested games. As you take each turn, follow the directions checked (✓) below.

☐ **Word:** Say each FL photo-word using your good FL sound.

☐ **Phrase:** Say each FL photo-word in the phrase "a ___ card."

☐ **Sentence:** Say each FL photo-word in the sentence "I have a ___ card."

***Tic-Tac-Toe*** - Players mark FL photo-words with **X**'s and **O**'s. Three in a row wins!
***Lotto*** - Helper calls out FL photo-words and player(s) cover(s) them with tokens/chips.
***Cards*** - Cut out the FL photo-words. Use them as flashcards.
***Memory*** - Make an extra copy, cut out photos, and play matching/memory games.

| | | |
|---|---|---|
| **flowers** | **fly** | **flashlight** |
| **flag** | **flat tire** | **float** |
| **flippers** | **flip flops** | **flame** |

_____   _____   _____
Name                                      Homework Helper                       Date         **FL**

# FL Puzzle Crossover

**Directions:** Read/say aloud each FL photo-word. As you draw a line from each photo-word to the word on the right that goes with it, follow the directions checked (✓) below.

- ☐ **Word:** Say each FL photo-word using your good FL sound.
- ☐ **Phrase:** Say each FL photo-word in the phrase "___ puzzle."
- ☐ **Sentence:** Say each FL photo-word in the sentence "I matched the ___ puzzle."

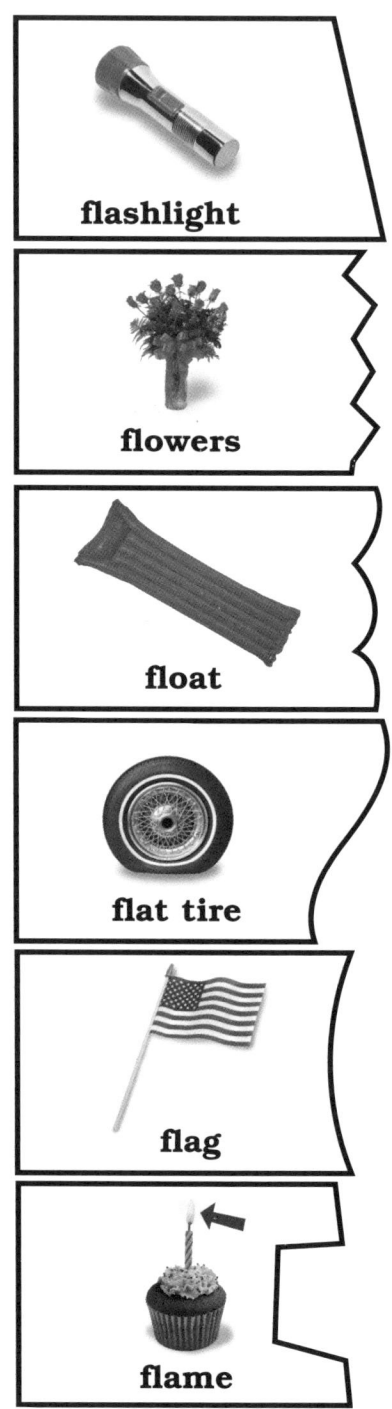
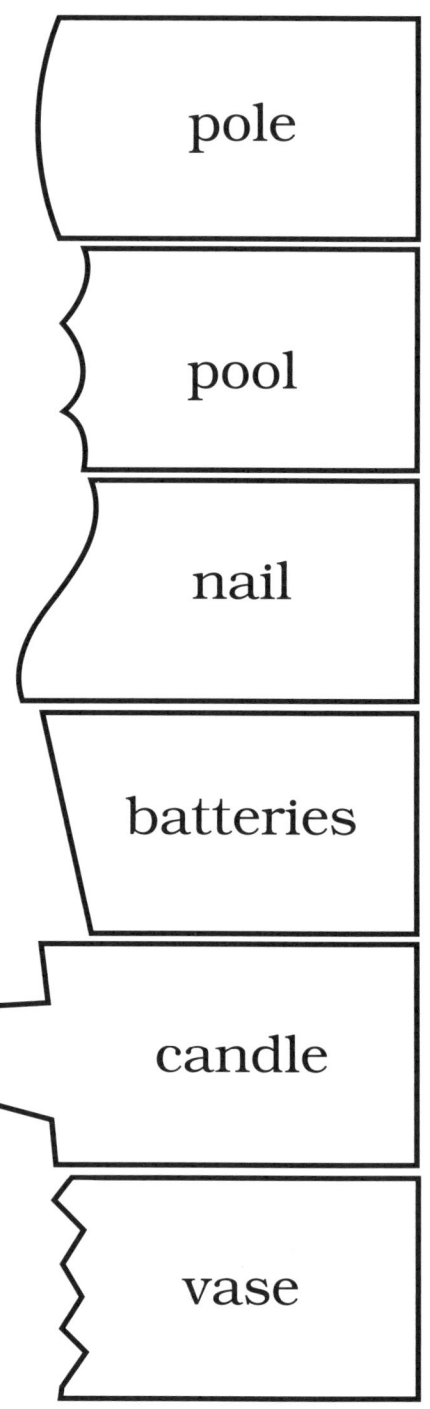

# Missing Vowel for FL

**Directions:** Read/say aloud each FL photo-word below. As you spell each word correctly by writing a vowel in the blank, follow the directions checked (✓) below.

- ☐ **Word:** Say each FL photo-word using your good FL sound.
- ☐ **Phrase:** Say each FL photo-word in the phrase "vowel in ___."
- ☐ **Sentence:** Say each FL photo-word in the sentence "I found a missing vowel in ___."

fl__g

flo__t

fl__ppers

fl__wers

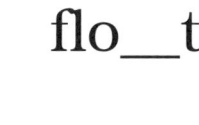

fl__p fl__ps

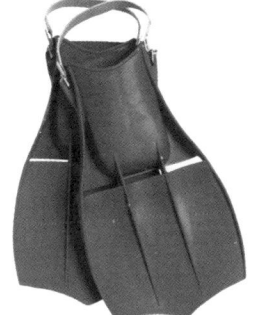

flashl__ght

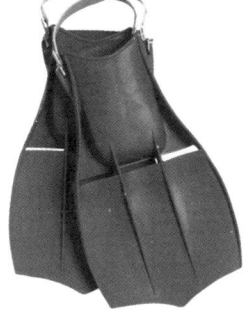

fl__me

fl__t t__re

Name _____  Homework Helper  Date _____  **FL**

# 4-in-1 for GL

**Directions:** Read/say aloud each GL photo-word below. Then, play one of the suggested games. As you take each turn, follow the directions checked (✓) below.

☐ **Word:** Say each GL photo-word using your good GL sound.

☐ **Phrase:** Say each GL photo-word in the phrase "a ___ card."

☐ **Sentence:** Say each GL photo-word in the sentence "I have a ___ card."

***Tic-Tac-Toe*** - Players mark GL photo-words with **X**'s and **O**'s. Three in a row wins!
***Lotto*** - Helper calls out GL photo-words and player(s) cover(s) them with tokens/chips.
***Cards*** - Cut out the GL photo-words. Use them as flashcards.
***Memory*** - Make an extra copy, cut out photos, and play matching/memory games.

| | | |
|---|---|---|
| **globe** | **glasses** | **glue** |
| **glitter** | **gloves** | **glazed doughnut** |
| **glass** | **glad** | **glamorous** |

Name _____   Homework Helper   Date _____   **GL**

# GL Listen and Follow

**Directions:** Read/say aloud each GL photo-word below. Use the photo-words for clues. As you answer each question, follow the directions checked (✓) below.

☐ **Word:** Say each GL photo-word using your good GL sound.

☐ **Phrase:** Say each GL photo-word answer in the phrase "mark ___."

☐ **Sentence:** Say each GL photo-word answer in the sentence "I marked the ___."

1. What keeps your hands warm? (Circle it.)

2. What is used to make things stick together? (Underline it.)

3. What helps you see? (Draw a square around it.)

4. What is round and has countries on it? (Draw an X on it.)

5. What holds ice and liquid? (Draw a star on it.)

6. What is sweet and has a hole in the center? (Draw a line through it.)

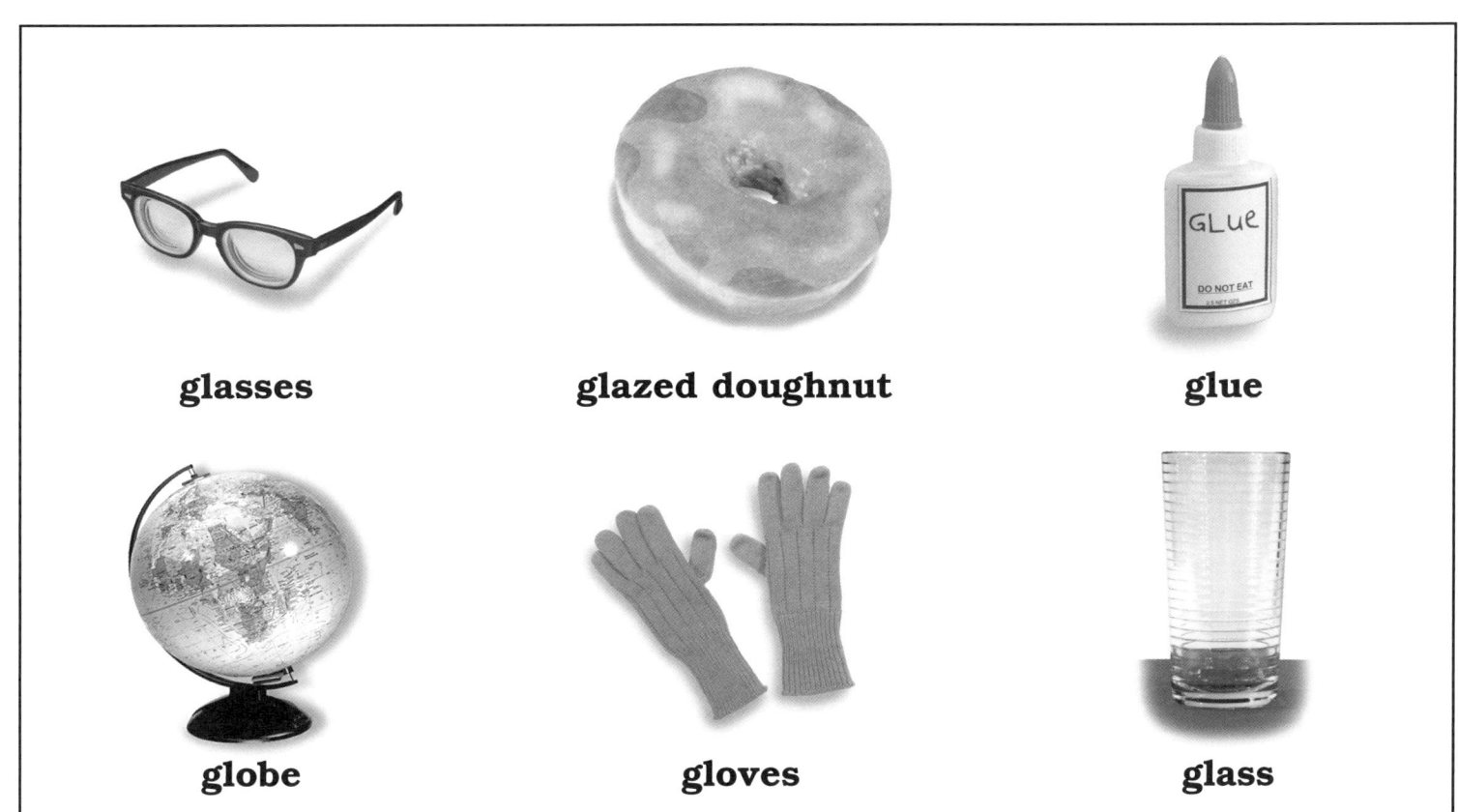

glasses     glazed doughnut     glue

globe     gloves     glass

# Secret GL Word

**Directions:** Read/say aloud each GL photo-word below. Using the Word Bank for clues, complete each sentence. As you write each answer, follow the directions checked (✓) below. Then, write and say the Secret Word.

- ☐ **Word:** Say each GL photo-word using your good GL sound.
- ☐ **Phrase:** Say each GL photo-word in the phrase "secret ___."
- ☐ **Sentence:** Say each GL photo-word as you read each complete sentence.

## Word Bank

glue   gloves   globe

glitter   glazed doughnut   glass

Answer key on page 32.

1. We found the oceans on the __ __ __ __ __ .
2. He used __ __ __ __ to fix his toy.
3. For our art project, the teacher gave us __ __ __ __ __ __ __ .
4. She ate a __ __ __ __ __ __   __ __ __ __ __ __ __ __ .
5. Before winter, he needs a new pair of __ __ __ __ __ __ .
6. There is a dirty __ __ __ __ __ in the sink.

**Secret Word:** ☐ ☐ ☐ ☐ ☐ ☐

# 4-in-1 for KL

**Directions:** Read/say aloud each KL photo-word below. Then, play one of the suggested games. As you take each turn, follow the directions checked (✓) below.

☐ **Word:** Say each KL photo-word using your good KL sound.

☐ **Phrase:** Say each KL photo-word in the phrase "a __ card."

☐ **Sentence:** Say each KL photo-word in the sentence "I have a __ card."

*Tic-Tac-Toe* - Players mark KL photo-words with **X**'s and **O**'s. Three in a row wins!
*Lotto* - Helper calls out KL photo-words and player(s) cover(s) them with tokens/chips.
*Cards* - Cut out the KL photo-words. Use them as flashcards.
*Memory* - Make an extra copy, cut out photos, and play matching/memory games.

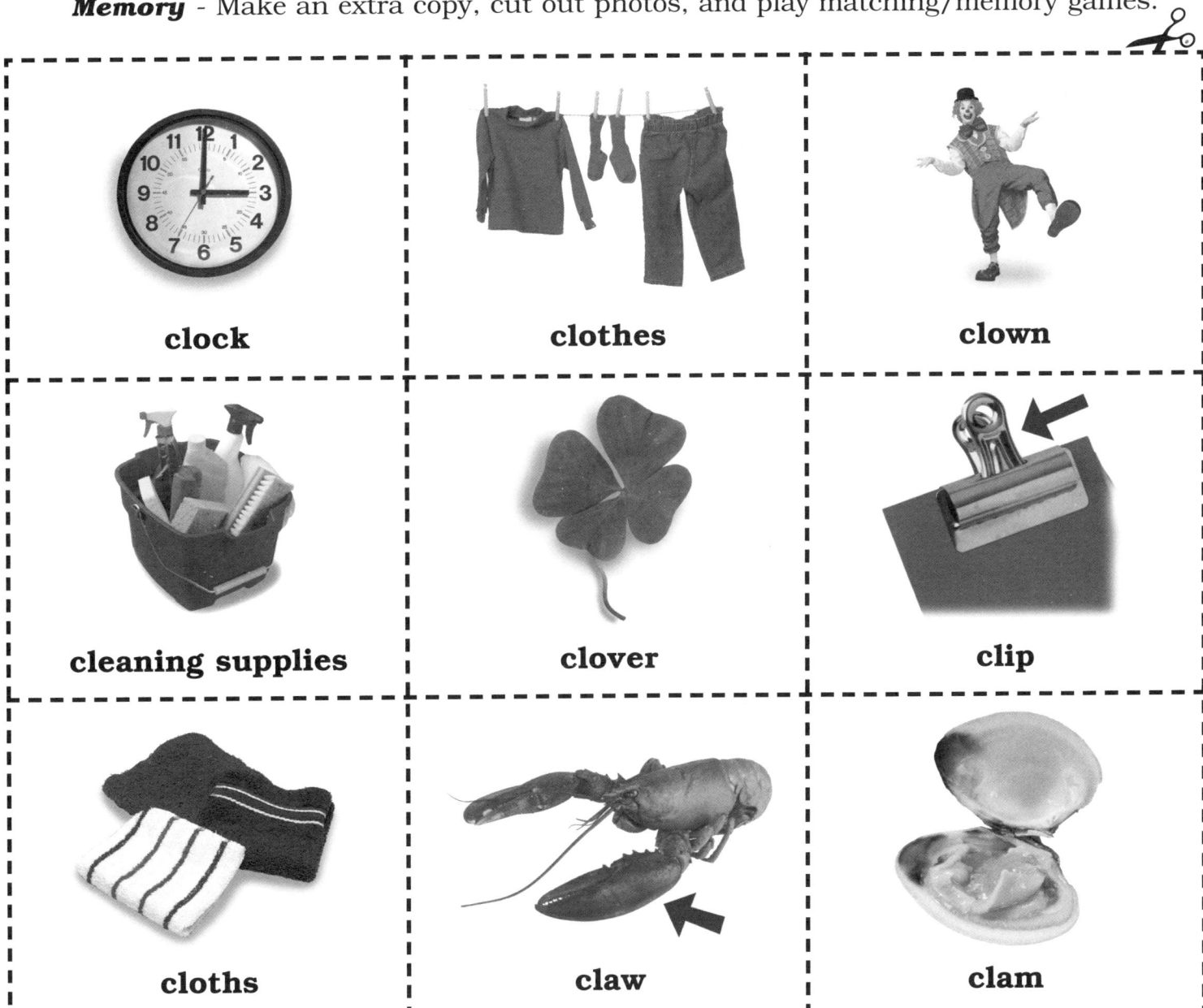

| clock | clothes | clown |
| cleaning supplies | clover | clip |
| cloths | claw | clam |

Name _____ Homework Helper _____ Date _____ KL

# Go-Together KL Match-Ups

**Directions:** Read/say aloud each KL photo-word on the left. Then, find the words that "Go Together." Draw a line from the photo-word in column "A" to the word in column "B" that goes together best. As you draw each line, follow the directions checked (✓) below.

☐ **Word:** Say each KL photo-word using your good KL sound.
☐ **Phrase:** Say each KL photo-word in the phrase "_____ and _____."
  <sub>A word    B word</sub>
☐ **Sentence:** Say each KL photo-word in the sentence "I drew a line from _____ to _____."
  <sub>A word    B word</sub>

**A**                    **B**

clip                     luck

clown                    mop

clock                    papers

clover                   shell

cleaning supplies        circus

clam                     numbers

Name _____  Homework Helper _____  Date _____  **KL**

# KL Paper Chain

**Directions:** Read/say aloud each KL photo-word below. Cut out the word strips. Turn them face down. Pick up a strip, and follow the directions checked (✓) below. When you are done, staple/glue the strips together to make a chain link.

- ☐ **Word:** Say each KL photo-word using your good KL sound.
- ☐ **Phrase:** Say each KL photo-word in the phrase "___ chain."
- ☐ **Sentence:** Say each KL photo-word in the sentence "___ is/are on my chain."

| | |
|---|---|
| claw | |
| clothes | |
| clown | |
| cleaning supplies | |
| clover | |
| clam | |

Name _____  Homework Helper  Date _____  KL

# 4-in-1 for PL

**Directions:** Read/say aloud each PL photo-word below. Then, play one of the suggested games. As you take each turn, follow the directions checked (✓) below.

- [ ] **Word:** Say each PL photo-word using your good PL sound.
- [ ] **Phrase:** Say each PL photo-word in the phrase "a ___ card."
- [ ] **Sentence:** Say each PL photo-word in the sentence "I have a ___ card."

*Tic-Tac-Toe* - Players mark PL photo-words with **X**'s and **O**'s. Three in a row wins!
*Lotto* - Helper calls out PL photo-words and player(s) cover(s) them with tokens/chips.
*Cards* - Cut out the PL photo-words. Use them as flashcards.
*Memory* - Make an extra copy, cut out photos, and play matching/memory games.

| | | |
|---|---|---|
| **pliers** | **playpen** | **plane** |
| **plug** | **plant** | **plum** |
| **plate** | **plunger** | **place mat** |

Name _____  Homework Helper  Date _____  **PL**

# PL Analogies

**Directions:** Read/say aloud each PL photo-word below. Read each analogy and fill in the correct answer from the Word Bank. Then, follow the directions checked (✓) below.

☐ **Word:** Say each PL photo-word using your good PL sound.

☐ **Phrase:** Say each PL photo-word in the phrase "is to ___."

☐ **Sentence:** Read each complete sentence below.

1. Food is to sandwich as tool is to _____.

2. Sails are to boat as wings are to _____.

3. Glass is to coaster as plate is to _____.

4. Vegetable is to carrot as fruit is to _____.

5. Jar is to jam as hanging basket is to _____.

6. Flashlight is to batteries as television is to _____.

7. Sleep is to crib as play is to _____.

8. Juice is to cup as hamburger is to _____.

## Word Bank

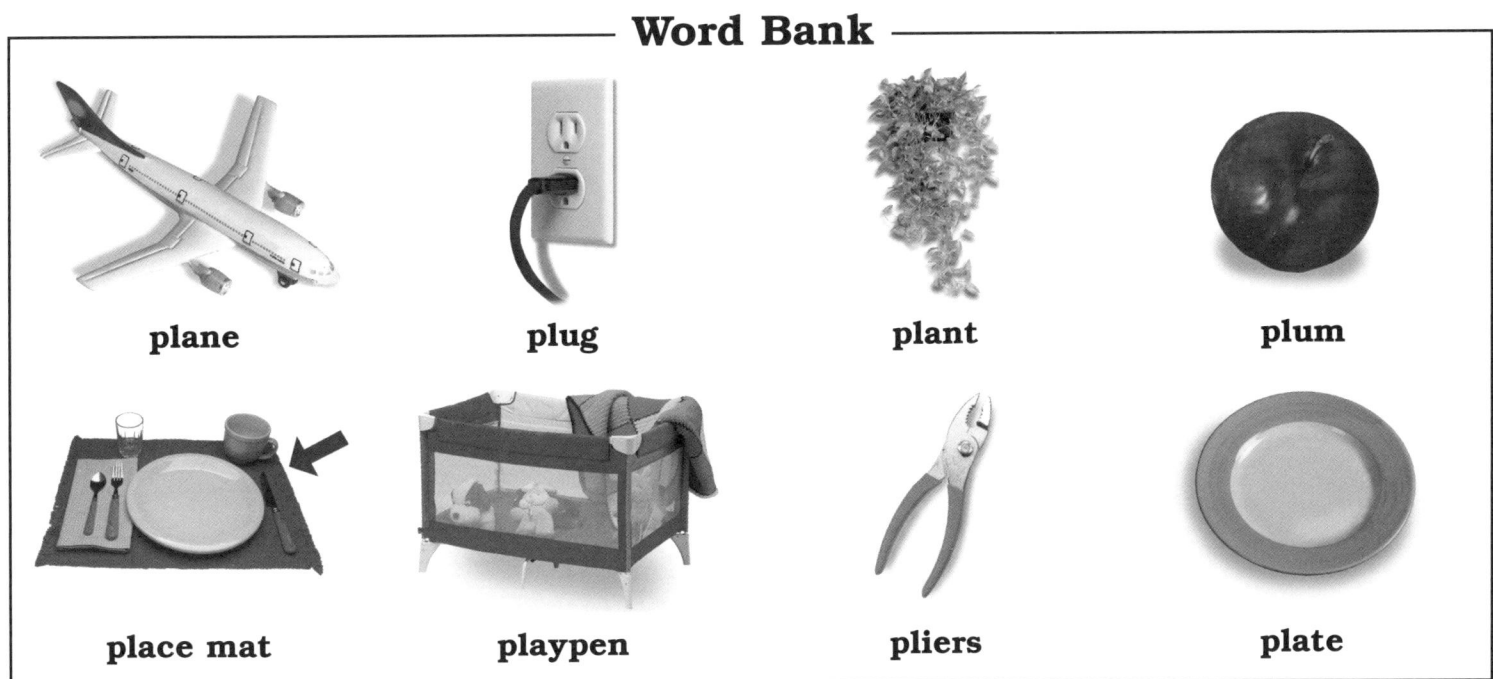

| plane | plug | plant | plum |
| place mat | playpen | pliers | plate |

Answer key on page 32.

Name _____    Homework Helper    Date _____    **PL**

# PL Crossword Fun

**Directions:** Read/say aloud each PL photo-word below. Use the words and the clues to complete the crossword puzzle. Then, follow the directions checked (✓) below.

☐ **Word:** Say each PL photo-word using your good PL sound.

☐ **Phrase:** Say each PL photo-word in the phrase "___ answer."

☐ **Sentence:** Say each PL photo-word in the sentence "My answer is ___."

plant

place mat

plane

playpen

plunger

plum

### Down
1. A fern.
2. A plate is placed on this.
4. A fruit.

### Across
2. A place for baby toys.
4. A tool for the toilet.
5. A vehicle with wings.

Answer key on page 32.

Name   Homework Helper   Date  **PL**

# 4-in-1 for SL

**Directions:** Read/say aloud each SL photo-word below. Then, play one of the suggested games. As you take each turn, follow the directions checked (✓) below.

☐ **Word:** Say each SL photo-word using your good SL sound.

☐ **Phrase:** Say each SL photo-word in the phrase "a ___ card."

☐ **Sentence:** Say each SL photo-word in the sentence "I have a ___ card."

*Tic-Tac-Toe* - Players mark SL photo-words with **X**'s and **O**'s. Three in a row wins!
*Lotto* - Helper calls out SL photo-words and player(s) cover(s) them with tokens/chips.
*Cards* - Cut out the SL photo-words. Use photos as flashcards.
*Memory* - Make an extra copy, cut out photos, and play matching/memory games.

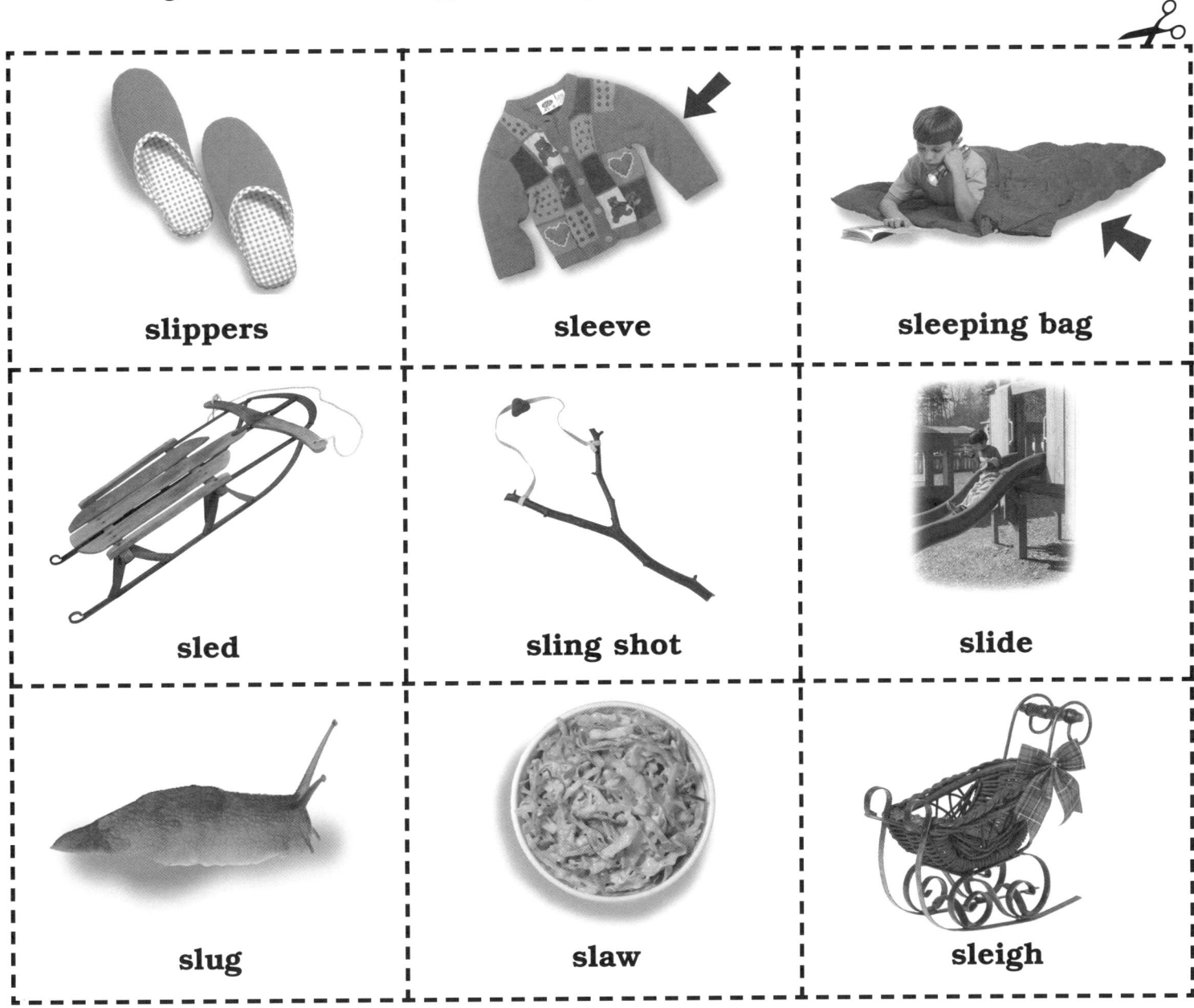

| slippers | sleeve | sleeping bag |
| sled | sling shot | slide |
| slug | slaw | sleigh |

Name _____  Homework Helper  Date _____  **SL**

# Toss the SL Cube

**Directions:** Read/say aloud each SL photo-word below. Assemble the cube: Glue onto construction paper if desired. Cut along the dotted lines. Fold on solid lines and glue. To play, toss the cube. As it lands with a photo-word face up, follow the directions checked (✓) below.

☐ **Word:** Say each SL photo-word using your good SL sound.

☐ **Phrase:** Say each SL photo-word in the phrase "___ side."

☐ **Sentence:** Say each SL photo-word in the sentence "It landed on ___."

Glue Tab C

slippers

Glue A | sleeve | sleeping bag | sled | Glue B

sling shot

Glue Tab A | slide | Glue Tab B

Glue C

Name     Homework Helper     Date     SL

# Word in an SL Word

**Directions:** Read/say aloud each SL photo-word below. Then, read the clues and find a word inside each photo-word (sunflower-low). As you write the "inside" word on each line, follow the directions checked (✓) below.

☐ **Word:** Say each SL photo-word using your good SL sound.

☐ **Phrase:** Say each SL photo-word in the phrase "(inside word) in ____"

☐ **Sentence:** Say each SL photo-word in the sentence "I found (inside word) in ____."

1. **sled** — Past tense of lead. _____

2. **slide** — Another word for a top. _____

3. **slippers** — The red part of your mouth. _____

4. **sling shot** — The opposite of cold. _____

5. **sleeping bag** — Ping Pong without the pong. _____

6. **sleeve** — A shortened word for evening. _____

Answer key on page 32.

Name _____  Homework Helper  Date _____  **SL**

# 4-in-1 for L Blends

**Directions:** Read/say aloud each L Blend photo-word below. Then, play one of the suggested games. As you take each turn, follow the directions checked (✓) below.

- ☐ **Word:** Say each L Blend photo-word using your good L Blend sound.
- ☐ **Phrase:** Say each L Blend photo-word in the phrase "a ___ card."
- ☐ **Sentence:** Say each L Blend photo-word in the sentence "I have a ___ card."

*Tic-Tac-Toe* - Players mark L Blend photo-words with **X**'s and **O**'s. Three in a row wins!
*Lotto* - Helper calls out L Blend photo-words and player(s) cover(s) them with tokens/chips.
*Cards* - Cut out the L Blend photo-words. Use photos as flashcards.
*Memory* - Make an extra copy, cut out photos, and play matching/memory games.

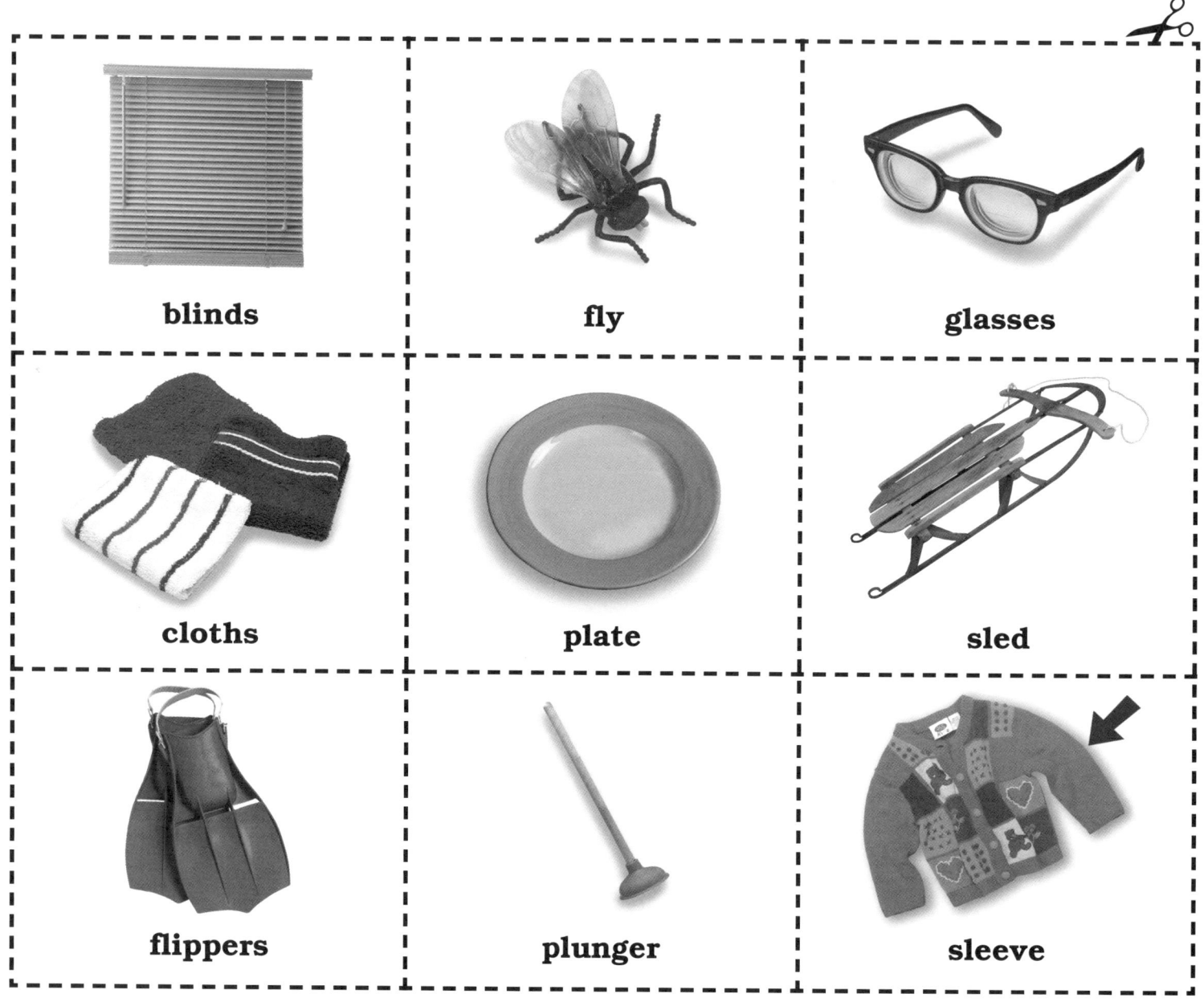

| blinds | fly | glasses |
| cloths | plate | sled |
| flippers | plunger | sleeve |

Name ___  Homework Helper  Date ___

**L Blends Combo**

# L Blend Word Search

**Directions:** Read/say aloud each L Blend photo-word below. Complete each phrase below, using the photo-words for clues. As you find and circle each answer in the puzzle, follow the directions checked (✓) below.

- ☐ **Word:** Say each L Blend photo-word using your good L Blend sound.
- ☐ **Phrase:** Say each L Blend photo-word in the phrase "find ____."
- ☐ **Sentence:** Say each L Blend photo-word in the sentence "I found ____."

**glad**

**clover**

**blanket**

**slide**

```
F F A T S H C F L O W E R S T
L R G H S M E E O T F K Y R F
A L K C L Q W F L R T T V U E
M K R O I J Y L H B L O C K S
E U N E D O W E R A V Z E P T
E R B D E A D C O N E M A E O
Z L L B S H E K G L A D D T E
V T A E A S U R E L I Y U O R
Z I N T S V Q E Y E T T Y E E
R M K U O C L X E A R F C K W
Y T E I C L C L E W U E T E E
H G T I L O E A R R A E O K Q
U M V L Y V P B P L A N T O F
P J Z J S E Y U C K T W I B E
L T S B O R S K Z B F T O P A
```

Answer key on page 32.

**flowers**

**flame**

**blocks**

**plant**

1. A warm _ _ _ _ _ _ _.
2. Vase of _ _ _ _ _ _ _.
3. Happy or _ _ _ _.
4. Four leaf _ _ _ _ _ _.
5. Water the _ _ _ _ _.
6. Go down the _ _ _ _ _.
7. Stack the _ _ _ _ _ _.
8. Blow out the _ _ _ _ _.

Name _____  Homework Helper  Date _____

**L Blends Combo**

# L Blend Mirror Image

**Directions:** Hold this page up to a mirror. Read aloud the words that appear. As you write each word correctly on the line, follow the directions checked (✓) below.

☐ **Word:** Say each L Blend photo-word using your good L Blend sound.

☐ **Phrase:** Say each L Blend photo-word in the phrase "see _____."

☐ **Sentence:** Say each L Blend photo-word in the sentence "I see a _____."

blouse _____

flag _____

glass _____

clock _____

plum _____

slug _____

place mat _____

float _____

glass

flag

slug

clock

blouse

place mat

plum

float

Name        Homework Helper        Date

**L Blends Combo**

# L Blends Rhyme Time

**Directions:** Read/say aloud each L Blend photo-word below. Then, next to each word listed below, write the rhyming photo-word. As you write, follow the directions checked (✓) below.

☐ **Word:** Say each L Blend photo-word using your good L Blend sound.

☐ **Phrase:** Say each L Blend photo-word in the phrase "___ and *(rhyming word)*."

☐ **Sentence:** Say each L Blend photo-word in the sentence "___ rhymes with *(rhyming word)*."

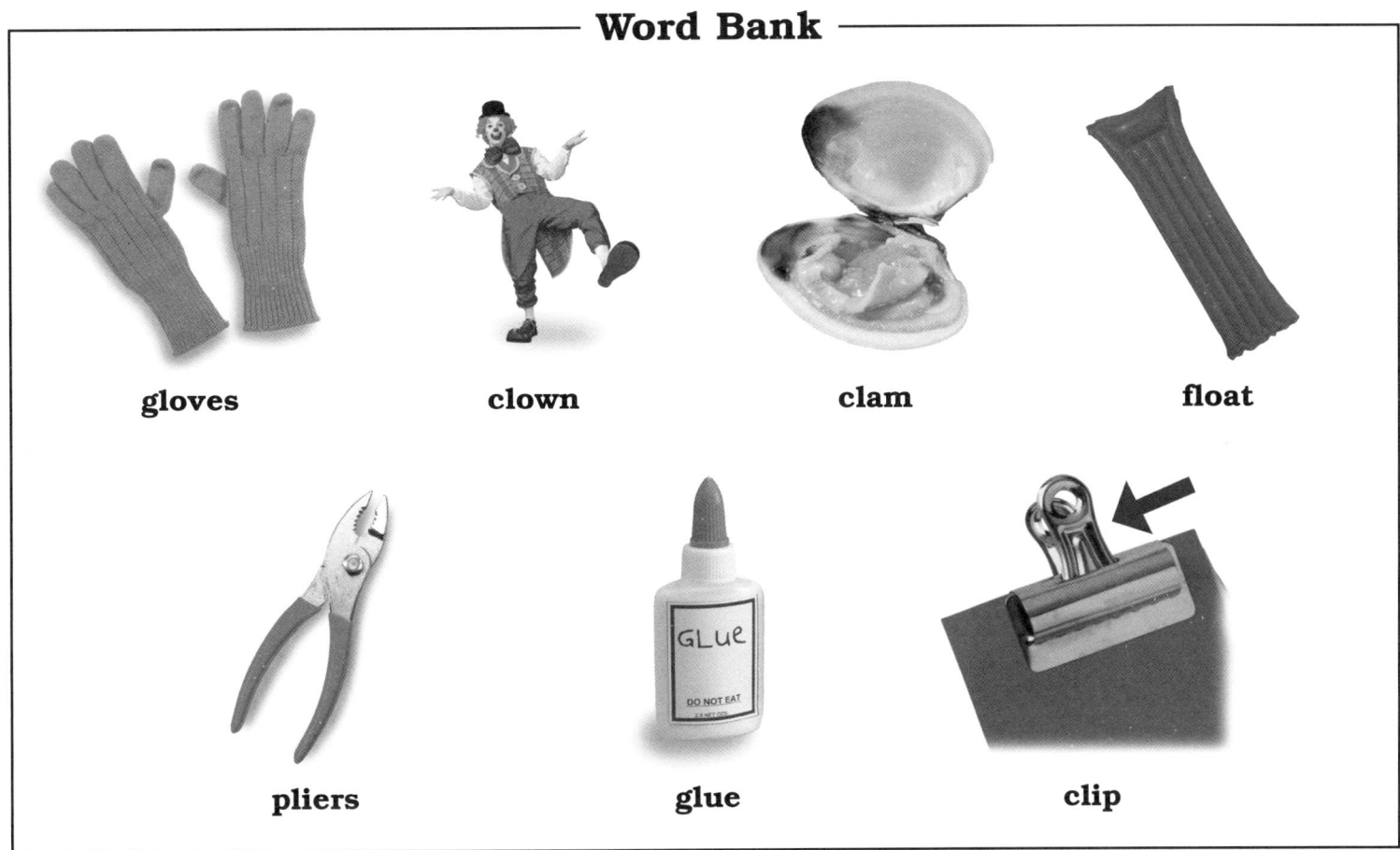

**Word Bank**

gloves   clown   clam   float

pliers   glue   clip

1. boat  _____

2. shoe  _____

3. down  _____

4. dip   _____

5. doves  _____

6. lamb   _____

7. dryers _____

Name _____   Homework Helper   Date _____

L Blends Combo

# L Blends Classify It

**Directions:** Read/say aloud each L Blend photo-word below. As you write a C below the clothes and an F below the food, follow the directions checked (✓) below.

- ☐ **Word:** Say each L Blend photo-word using your good L Blend sound.
- ☐ **Phrase:** Say each L Blend photo-word in the phrase "my ___."
- ☐ **Sentence:** Say each L Blend photo-word in the sentence "My ___ is/are in the right category."

| C Clothes | F Food |

**plum**

**blueberries**

**gloves**

_____   _____   _____

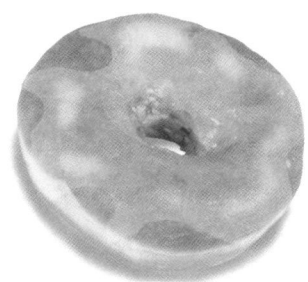

**glazed doughnut**

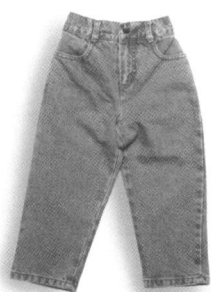

**blue jeans**

**flip flops**

_____   _____   _____

Name     Homework Helper     Date

**L Blends Combo**

# Box One L Blend

**Directions:** Read/say aloud each L Blend photo-word below. Then, read each statement. As you draw a box around each correct answer, follow the directions checked (✓) below.

- ☐ **Word:** Say each L Blend photo-word using your good L Blend sound.
- ☐ **Phrase:** Say each L Blend photo-word in the phrase "the ___."
- ☐ **Sentence:** Say each L Blend photo-word in the sentence "It is the ___."

1. Draw a box around the one that is used in a classroom.

   flat tire     blackboard

2. Draw a box around the one that is found on a lobster.

   claw     plug

3. Draw a box around the one that is worn with a robe.

   slippers     flip flops

4. Draw a box around the one that has a ladder.

   playpen     slide

5. Draw a box around the one that uses batteries.

   flame     flashlight

Name     Homework Helper     Date     L Blends Combo

# L Blends Circle, Draw and Say

**Directions:** Read/say aloud each L Blend photo-word below. Then, read the sentences. Circle one picture to complete each sentence. Then tell the whole story using your good L Blend sound.

Cloe the Clumsy Clown went to the playground to ride on the...

slide.                     sled.

On her way there, she had a...

   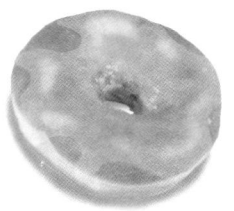

flat tire.                 glazed doughnut.

While playing, she ripped a hole in her...

sleeve.                    blouse.

She decided next time, she would carry her lucky...

clover.                    blanket.

Name _____ Homework Helper _____ Date _____

# Relatively Speaking

**Directions**: Read/say aloud each L Blend photo-word below. Then, finish the story. Use at least five words from the Word Bank in the story. Then, read/say the story aloud, using your good L Blend sound.

## Word Bank

| fly | plant | playpen | clothes |
|---|---|---|---|
| blueberries | flowers | sleeping bag | glasses |

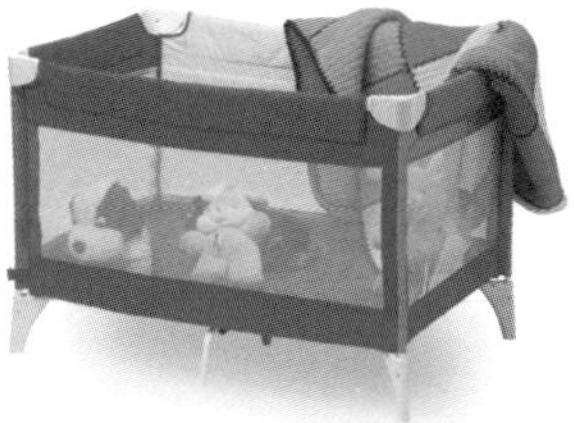

Blimpy, the black sheep, lost his favorite blanket. While searching for his blanket with a flashlight, Blimpy saw...

_____

_____

_____

_____

_____

Name _____  Homework Helper  Date _____

**L Blends Carryover**

# L Blends Conversation Strips

**Directions:** Read/say aloud each L Blend photo-word below. Then, cut apart the strips and place them face down. Choose a strip and talk about each one using at least five (5) sentences in your answer. For more L Blend fun, choose another strip.

---

Would you rather be a (fly) or a (slug)? Why?

---

Describe a (clown).

---

You find a magic (clover) that gives you three wishes. What will they be? Why?

---

You have a remote controlled (float). Where do you go and what do you see?

---

You have a dream about winning a (blue ribbon). Describe the dream.

---

Name _____ Homework Helper _____ Date _____

**L Blends Carryover**

# L Blends Story Loop

**Directions:** Read/say aloud each L Blend photo-word below. Cut out the circles. Glue/tape or place any circles you wish on the story loop. Then, go around the loop and tell a story, using these L Blend words. When you are done, mix up the words and tell another story!

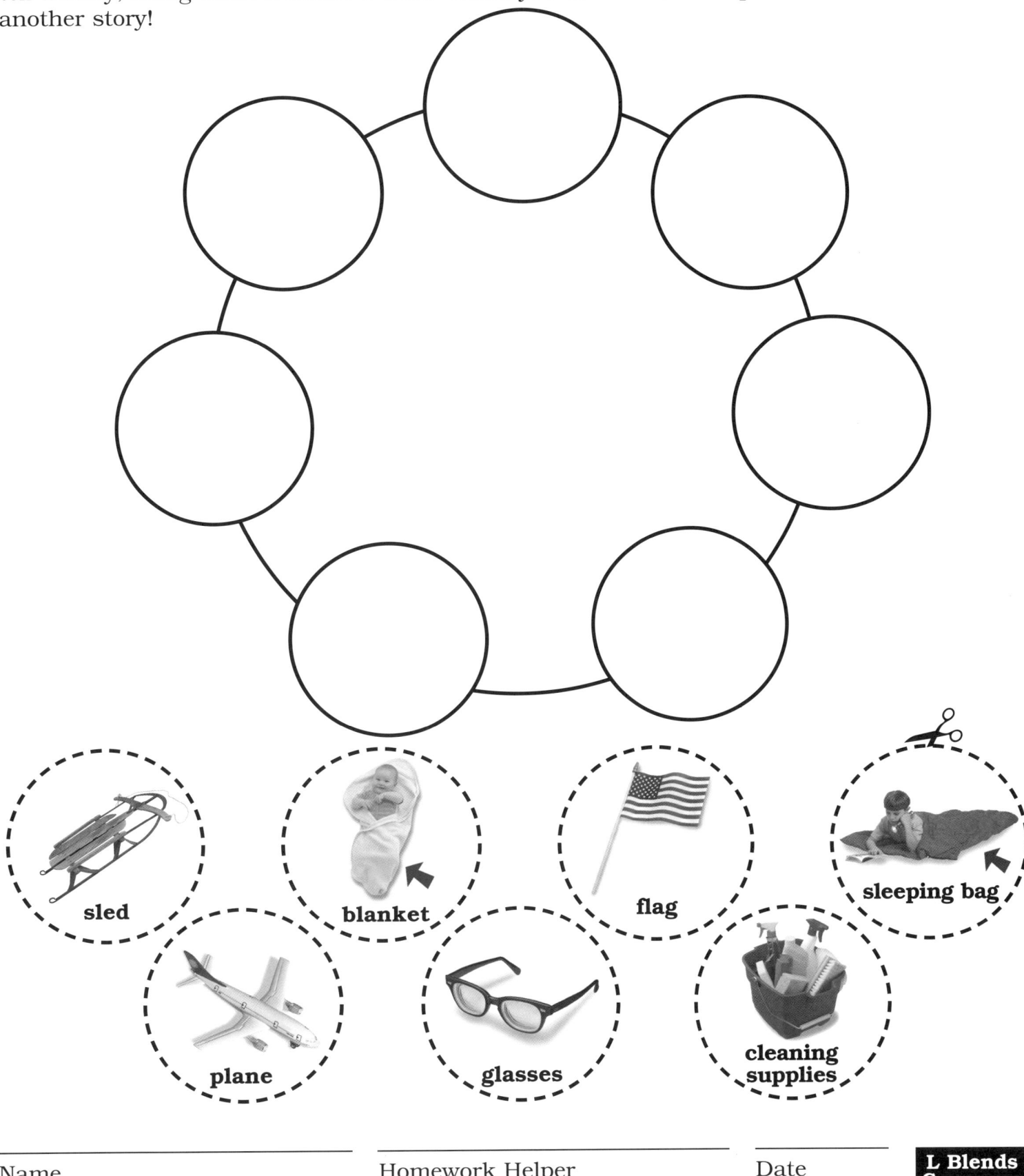

sled • blanket • flag • sleeping bag • plane • glasses • cleaning supplies

# L Blends Same and Different

**Directions:** Read/say aloud each L Blend photo-word below. Then, tell how the words in the word pairs below are the same and how they are different. Use your good L Blend sound!

1.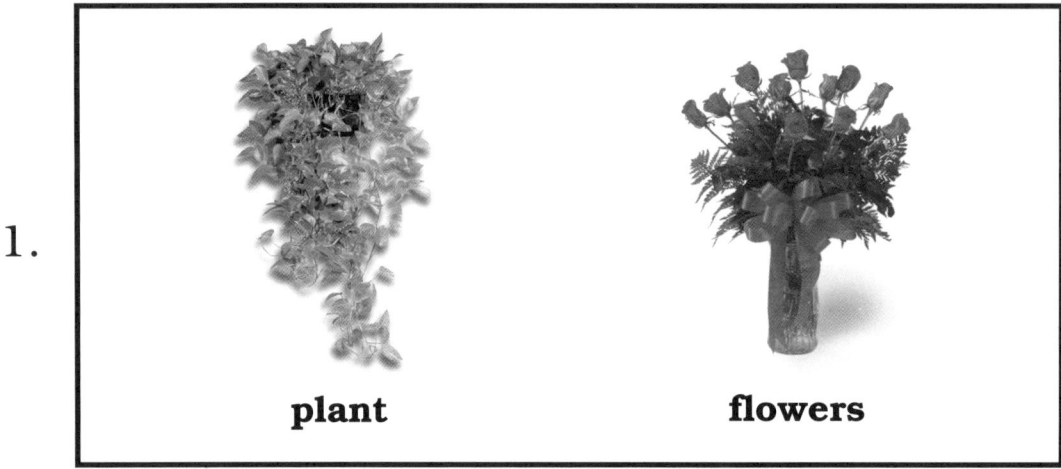
   **plant**  **flowers**

2.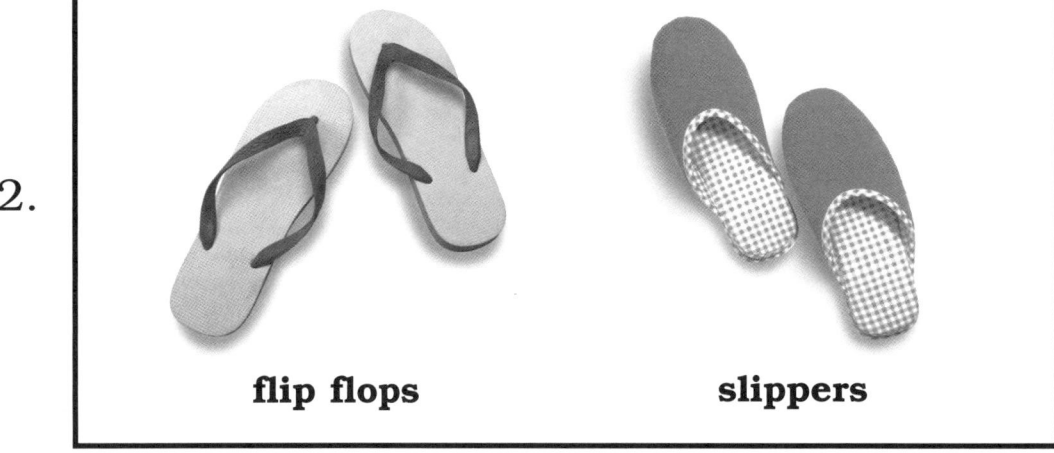
   **flip flops**  **slippers**

3.
   **flashlight**  **flame**

# Silly L Blends Story

**Directions:** Read/say aloud each L Blend photo-word below. Then, cut out the pictures. Place them face down. Choose a picture and glue/tape or place it in an open space in the story. After all pictures are placed in the story, read your Silly Story, using your good L Blend sound.

    Florence the Flamingo loves to dance in her ☐. She is so excited because tonight she gets to dance with Glenda, the glamorous ☐. Her classmates are planning a surprise party for her, in which a/the ☐ will jump out of a/the ☐. After the show, "The Blue Moon," everyone claps and throws a/the ☐. When the long night is over, Florence the Flamingo falls asleep with her ☐.

| playpen | slug | clown | sleeping bag | slippers | flowers |

# You win the Blue Ribbon for your L Blends!

_____
Presented to

_____        _____
Speech-Language Pathologist                Date

## Activity Answers:

**Pg 10**   1. g<u>l</u>obe, 2. g<u>l</u>ue, 3. g<u>l</u>itter,
4. g<u>l</u>azed doughnut, 5. g<u>l</u>ove<u>s</u>,
6. g<u>l</u>as<u>s</u> (Secret Word: glides)

**Pg 15**   1. pliers, 2. plane, 3. place mat,
4. plum, 5. plant, 6. plug,
7. playpen, 8. plate

**Pg 16**   **Down:** 1. plant, 2. place mat, 4. plum
**Across:** 2. playpen, 4. plunger, 5. plane

**Pg 19**   1. led, 2. lid, 3. lip,
4. hot, 5. ping, 6. eve

**Pg 21**

| F | F | A | T | S | H | C | F | L | O | W | E | R | S | T |
|---|---|---|---|---|---|---|---|---|---|---|---|---|---|---|
| L | R | G | H | S | M | E | E | O | T | F | K | Y | R | F |
| A | L | K | C | L | Q | W | F | L | R | T | T | V | U | E |
| M | K | R | O | I | J | Y | L | H | B | L | O | C | K | S |
| E | U | N | E | D | O | W | E | R | A | V | Z | E | P | T |
| E | R | B | D | E | A | D | C | O | N | E | M | A | E | O |
| Z | L | L | B | S | H | E | K | G | L | A | D | D | T | E |
| V | T | A | E | A | S | U | R | E | L | I | Y | O | R |
| Z | I | N | T | S | V | Q | E | Y | E | T | T | Y | E | E |
| R | M | K | U | O | C | L | X | E | A | R | F | C | K | W |
| Y | T | E | I | C | L | C | L | E | W | U | E | T | E | E |
| H | G | T | I | L | O | E | A | R | R | A | E | O | K | Q |
| U | M | V | L | Y | V | P | B | P | L | A | N | T | O | F |
| P | J | Z | J | S | E | Y | U | C | K | T | W | I | B | E |
| L | T | S | B | O | R | S | K | Z | B | F | T | O | P | A |